T0339097

SKY = EMPTY

New Issues Poetry & Prose

Editor   William Olsen

Managing Editor   Marianne Swierenga

Copy Editor   Kory M. Shrum

Assistant Editors   Andrea England, Natalie Giarratano, Jonathan
                      Rice, and Chad Sweeney

New Issues Poetry & Prose
The College of Arts and Sciences
Western Michigan University
Kalamazoo, MI 49008

First Edition, 2010.

ISBN-10   1-930974-91-4 (paperbound)
ISBN-13   978-1-930974-91-3 (paperbound)

Library of Congress Cataloging-in-Publication Data:
Halebsky, Judy
Sky = Empty/Judy Halebsky
Library of Congress Control Number: 2009939910

Art Director   Barbara Loveland
Designer   Nico Curtis
Production Manager   Paul Sizer
                      The Design Center, Frostic School of Art
                      College of Fine Arts
                      Western Michigan University
Printing: McNaughton & Gunn, Inc.

SKY=EMPTY

Judy Halebsky

New Issues Press

WESTERN MICHIGAN UNIVERSITY

how many languages does a pear tree speak?
—Roy Kiyooka

Contents

Acknowledgments

Thanks to the editors of the following publications where some of these poems, or their earlier versions were published:

Anteup: "The Sears and Roebuck House"
The Antigonish Review: "Eve's talking about Dylan"
Eleven Eleven {1111}: "Whale Music"
Five Fingers Review: "Folksong (translation)" and "Oh sky, a little bit even, fly not"
Grain Magazine: "Musquodoboit Harbour" and "Aunt Tory is always getting cold"
High Desert Journal: "Woman Under Trees"
Mamazine: "On the Coast," "Passing" published as "The Big School"
New Delta Review: "Purcell's Cove Road" and "École Beaufort"
Ping Pong: "The Kite Maker"
Poetry Now: "Thinned by Storm"
Rattlesnake Press, Broadside: "her heart sounds" "Glossary (spoken)," and "Daddy says he teaches people about people"
Squaw Valley Review: "Butter Melts in Summer"
Tertulia: "Prognosis" and "Out of the Nest"

Poems from this collection are included in a 20 page, limited edition chapbook titled: *Japanese for Daydreamers* published by Finishing Line Press, 2008.

Poems from this collection are also included in the anthology *Yuba Flows*, edited by Gail Entrekin and published by Hip Pocket Press, 2007.

(cont.)

It is thanks to the poets of the Sacramento Poetry Center's Tuesday night workshop that this manuscript took shape. I am grateful for their encouragement, guidance, and friendship. And to my CPC teacher and guide at Davis who on many days kept me upright and facing forward. I am indebted to the MacDowell Colony and the Millay Colony for their wonderful support and also to the workshops at Squaw Valley Community of Writers and the Port Townsend Writers' Conference.

空 Sky = Empty

お空はちょっとも飛べない
Oh Sky, a little bit even, fly not

You can move between French and English
put the table in the kitchen
and the soft red chair by the window

but with Japanese you can't bring what you already have
like the words: me, you
or how to count: 1 bed, 2 chairs, 3 days

an airplane takes off from Sacramento
I lie at an angle so I can see the fig tree out the window

arms for wings
ears for songs
3 days for water
sleep for sleep
chocolate for chocolate
vodka for vodka
kanji for death
death for surrender
surrender for sleep and 10,000 years

the sky is (o for honorific)
a little bit (silent syllable) even
(I (implied) cannot fly

I cannot fly in the sky at all

嫯 Woman Under Trees

it's the harvest Mom says
work night and day
so there'll be food in the winter
she's talking about me and homework
and trying to graduate

suede sneakers and bay windows
you would find me
a couple bars under healthy
in the bedroom too small
with all the noise from the street

you might think these aren't my words
not my body, not sounds that shaped me
when I was growing through shadows on the wall

> 海女   *ama*
> ocean woman:
> a woman diving for shells

> 姦   *kan*
> three women:
> wickedness and mischief

> 雨女   *ameonna*
> rain woman:
> a woman who brings rain

these words flood into the river
they are trees that rise uprooted
they are butterflies in the trees

Folksong (translation)

In Portuguese they have a specific verb
for throwing something out the window

that was after, right now I'm making your shadow
tracing your movements
catching the sharp edges
the consonants, cross outs, catch phrases, latchkey, house key
wearing its shape into the change purse of my wallet
I'm keeping it there in case I need to go back
unlock those four summers, the piles of stones, pass my fingers
over the Braille of incomplete sentences

the fields near your house in Connemara
are this lush misty green with mazes of stone walls
four feet high like an outline of city windows
not walls to make rooms or to mark off space
just walls as a place to pile the stones

in Japanese there is one character
that means searching for something
and a different character
that means searching for something that you lost

I try to imagine farming in those little boxes
with no openings for a plow
no doorways, no spaces for coming or going
he's writing us in 500 word news clips
he's typing us in squares across the field

incredible is the same word in French and English
when you say it in San Francisco it means unbelievably wonderful
when you say it in Quebec City it means unbelievably wicked

letters for me still come to your house
they won't bring me back or let you go
they write out the words: ice floe, glacier, granite
drainpipe, folksong, doorway

I Remember Her in Myrrh in Amber

She is waving the bus to stop
with both hands

she is searching for her glasses
on the beach in the dark

> 忘れる
> rush + heart:
> to forget

the old church at 10th and Mission

a stretch limo in white

the sun in December

she is waving the bus to stop with both hands

Water Voices

to Anatole Lubovich, poet and translator, 1937-2005

I will only say that poets are like trees:
they are all united by their roots in the earth
and their branches in the sky
      —Claude Roy

水心   a water heart
         means how to swim

how to make yourself float
how to be light enough to laugh
to float when it's already dark
and the doctors have their Xs and Os
and the birds are already south
and the leaves have fallen to puddles

how to float with no mooring
the jasmine in Berkeley in December
the gingko leaves yellow in all corners of the street
the way we prop ourselves up to dawn

水人   water people:
         what you tried to carry

水話   water voices:
         the sound of water

水人話 water people talking:
         a love song

My Father Remembers Blue Zebras

He remembers that he lost his wallet

he knows about the rainshadow
and the string of islands off the coast of Vancouver

覚える
oboeru   to remember
                also means to learn

I try to keep track of what he put where
the small green car we called Cricket
the second time he got drafted
and Aunt Nina's husband, *he's a nice guy but he's a fascist*

he's asking me again
where do you live
oh, you're in school, what do you study

how far off coast do you have to go
to be sheltered from the rain

that's wonderful Dad says, *that's wonderful*

Zen Monks Talking Big

稲妻に悟らぬ人の貴さよ
　—Basho

inazuma ni
satoranu hito no
tattosa yo

Basho played softball, second base
he also slept with the nuns and had to leave town
drank sake in rice fields
talked to spiders and half moons and cobwebs
laughed at the rain getting his sleeping mat wet

watching the lightning
those who share simply
are noble

inazuma (lightning) ni (with)
satora (enlightened, realized) nu (not) hito (people) no
(possessive)
tattosa (honorable, noble) yo (yo)

I repeat: yo means yo

highbrow talk
over the lightning
such a pity

Thinned by Storm

You might think that *kamikaze* means suicide pilot
but really it's a way of not saying something
a way of counting what's missing

> *Kami—god*
> *Kaze—wind*
> *Divine wind*
> *God of the wind*
> *God of the trees*

I'm counting on my fingers
on my toes
tracing the patterns on my skin
the blood lines, the needles, the nurses

worse than this the man on the radio says
is to be a parent to someone equally wounded

to my mother, I hand over the long nights
in pounds of salt, in gray canvas, in folded sheets

my swollen joints
layers of chalk skin

I should protect her
I should tell her it doesn't hurt at all

instead, leaves fall around us
as we walk in the park

Down the Mountain

Take me as nothing left
lift me twisted through granite and moss
water lung, milk waist, sage
I pass through these pages like a ghost

erase my shape in the sun on the porch
brown my skin into the riverbed
push my words into a lullaby
paper lung
milk waist and sage
whatever I came with exhausted
I pass through these pages like a ghost
whatever I came with I spent

Whale Music

Whale Music

I.

There are paper maps of fishing routes
the gulf stream, the whale surfacing areas

you make a map of the days in between

these are numbers you need for the map:
68, 63, 60, 56, 42, 40, 50

then you'll need a string tied to a nail
now you can make lines, measure distance, think about
proportions

like how much water there is in the ocean
how many fish there used to be
and how big a whale is compared to a human body

these are the words you need for the map:
Atlantic cod, fishing rights, gully, bank, 100 fathoms

Roseway, LaHave, Canso
Sydney Island
St. Johns
Hamilton Inlet

fathom: to determine the depth of sound
fathom: to find the nature of
fathom: to measure the depth of the ocean

II.

Fish houses, coast guard, longitude
they surface now and then
out the window down the bay we can see
a dark shiny stretch coming up in the water

mica straining whale music, lobster traps, sardines

we'll walk out and watch from far away
we'll spend a few hours or the whole afternoon
watching the whales breathe

mica straining, lobster traps, sardines

lawn fertilizers drain into the ocean
collect in their blubber
in their kidneys and liver
as they're straining fish through their horse hair teeth
pulling in mica and cod and seaweed

fathom: to measure the depth of the ocean
fathom: to determine the nature of
fathom: to hear the sound of whales

III.

Late August out on the porch in Lunenburg
laughing, drinking, beer bottles and cheese bread

draw a line across the page
this is the ground

whale music—that's what he called it
the man who made music to summon the whales

re-trace the line across the page
this is the sky

draw a small line at an angle
this is the coastline
it goes into the ocean
the ocean goes

fathom: callused hands pulling in nets
fathom: to know the nature of
fathom: to measure loss

Relativity

Mom says Stalin was a Bad Communist

They get me to climb to high branches
to drop the apples down
thanksgiving in the valley and rows and rows of trees
Daddy bites off, then spits out the bad spots of my apple
and hands it back to me

[1941] the ceilings were low, the apartments crowded

Grandmother pulls on her heavy skirt, pushes out the wrinkles
men wear button down shirts and shake hands, put their arms
around each other

everyone comes over to eat and visit and there's all this talking
mostly about things I don't know, like Spain and Stalin
and the army corps of engineers

Daddy got into Bronx Science, he knows how to measure and
how to weigh small small things, like a sperm and egg
mist on the window, or a breath of air

Grandmother sews sequins on dresses

[1911] the ceilings were low, the apartments crowded

they could only get one child on the boat
Grandmother's sister Bella, the oldest, was supposed to go
but she got scared or maybe fell in love, maybe
she didn't understand that the days were piling up
that the days were leaning together, that it would get worse

Eve got married and I walked down the aisle dropping flowers

Grandmother sewing sequins on dresses one by one by one

they're looking and looking but it's too small to see
so they guess and guess again

what's inside an atom and what's it going
to take to split it in half and in half again
heavy water, uranium, a handful of tenured professors
train trips, relativity, cigarettes

my father in a lab coat at City College
measuring the distance from here to Cuba in strokes

(notes on why)

they were trying to make a bomb
and they had this guy Heisenberg
who understood uncertainty and particles
and the chances of what would move where

this was after relativity
where light bends around a door
and things that seem to happen at the exact same time
actually happen at different times

Nagasaki depends on the angle
on how you measure
Manchuria, soldiers, civilians and God

dear Jessie, I'm trying to calculate the chances

measure him out in probability
but it's not looking good
there's an infinite number of things that can happen
and no one knows why out of all the options
only one gets pinned down into the present moment

and on top of that
being together at the same space in time and location
depends on where you're looking from

and it gets worse
because time changes with how fast you travel
so you might feel like it was just a week ago
but the same week for him could be three years
and by now he's woken up without you
almost a thousand times

木
tree

霊
ghost

木　霊
tree　ghost

木霊
echo

Across from Carl's Jr.
at 5th and Covell
there's a huge old tree
in an empty field on my way to school

while the BBC translates
while satellites measure
while troops are moving
while lives are counted out into matching piles
and brides in Sacramento try on dresses

white
and a size too small

I am looking at this tree

Seabass Blackbass Rockbass

Musquodoboit Harbour

standing waist deep in the current collecting
pressed fall leaves, rain boots,   sparrow grass,   bridge
street   in a tight sealed jar

one onethousand two onethousand three onethousand
to keep the blankets over us   Mike catches   two slow breaths
silverjumper rivermouthsalmon

quillback rockfish needlefish   in these waters   once

Mike catches   bigger than Allison's eight month baby
five onethousand six onethousand seven onethousand

water in the lungs   grasscarp stoneroller bonefish
trying to move them   over
where the strong boats with knots and men
fished to money and made the waters dry

Forestside Crescent

The houses on my street hang together like dolls
my Daddy always talks in threes

the man with the mustache asks me questions
do you dream in color? do you dream in black and white?

sleep dream, eyes closed dream, bus home dream, try to sleep dream
which dream

the boy in #36, his dad went to live with a woman on the highway
he went and took the TV, Mom said that was an awful Daddy
to take the TV

putting leaves red and yellow on wax paper
collecting chestnuts in a bag
everything in boxes
into a white truck

my Daddy always talks in threes because the words are too big
because I get lost in all the spaces

Mom tried to get me a kitten for my birthday, but I was afraid to
hold it and Maya sneezed and had to stay up in her room so we
gave it back to the lady

Daddy always talks in threes and puts cinnamon in oatmeal
he wants to know the pattern the branches make against the sky
he wants to know

my lips are sealed like the toenail moon
my street holds together like paper dolls

the man with the mustache has a wife and a piano and I get to
play it but she yells down the stairs   *not so hard   not so hard*

École Beaufort

Madame Caya likes to talk about God, everyday she likes to. she says she's not afraid to die, she says J'ai hâte which means—you can't exactly say back in English, the translation never fits, school talk and home talk are different. most words can't change, they don't fit in the other one, school is through the gate. I fit in like a row of dolls, I pile in the line, except for letters, all the rows of letters, they never go together, they never make sounds or words, they just stay letters.

Daddy told me to tell the teacher I don't pray. say that I have to go stand outside when they say the prayer. he made me promise I would. and every morning when we stand up to say Our Father I don't think about the words I think about what Daddy said, how I'm not supposed to be there, how we don't do that, how they can't make me, how I'm supposed to stand outside, how I'm the kid in the hall, sent out of the room, that's me except now right now I just slide my lips over the words trying to look like everyone else.

to see if we could
see if we could throw a ball over our flat roof house

a man came to fix the roof and said to my mom
there's about fifty tennis balls up there, you want 'em

Passing

Daddy uses big words
because no one understands
he failed kindergarten with glasses and earaches
and Fanny shouting into the phone
who fails kindergarten?

he learned English like a math test
with a thousand variables
calculations, equations, limitless permutations

Maya wants to go to college
so she's learning words out of a book for the test
pedantic—using really big words for no reason
tortuous—extra super complicated
cloyed—to eat so much chocolate you just can't eat any more

she says she's heard them all before from Daddy
but she never knew what he meant
about her insipid pop music
her Friday night mendacity
her teenage ennui

Eve's talking about Dylan
and marriage
and how he yells and yells
that's why they watch TV
so he won't yell
they watch every night
and Eve says
there's nothing good on

Monster Walking in a Snowstorm with Feet Tied Together

Mr. Spencer met my dad
and he's still laughing
saying *you're your daddy's girl*
your daddy's girl
shakes his head and laughs

and I just know Daddy came in all excited
and talked and talked and talked
loud like New York and everyone else
froze still, stood back and stared
but he doesn't notice
just keeps right on
about what is terrible and wonderful
warm and desolate

Mr. Spencer can't believe it either
what does your dad do
when did he move here

Daddy comes to get me after school
sees Mr. Spencer and my painting

Daddy thinks it's really something special
he keeps asking Mr. Spencer what he thinks
if he can see it too, the special something about it
the blue snow or monster feet
Mr. Spencer smiling wide and nodding

Mr. Spencer says, *your dad*, and smiles real big
your dad, and laughs

Glossary (spoken)

Vera's telling it all the long way
and saying yup on the inhale
like a hiccup or chin nod

she tells it to me the way they do
over in Newfoundland
so the words
are kind of lopsided

like being lonely as a gull on a rock
or three days older than the fog
and molasses-y bread that's right good
right some good
and Valerie finishing high school

we'll see about that now we will

Daddy's shouting *he's a fascist, he's a fascist*

Husband 3 is not perfect
but we try to get along
because Aunt Nina was too hard to handle
for the other ones
shaking her finger at me
I married for love, each time

she and husband 3 joined that club for people with high IQs
they have potlucks and trade recipes
and talk to other really smart people

Daddy gives a long slow breath out
says it's a club for people who could have done something

Bronx highway, sewing machine, birdcage
he sees years ago, Aunt Nina, a dancer
with jazz shoes, tap shoes and callused feet

what Daddy really wants to know
is if a fascist can have such a high IQ

the other girls, they married doctors
shaking her finger at me again
and that was no mistake

a fascist, I don't really know what that means
but Daddy says it about husband 3 when he's angry
yells it loud and spits
then later he says it all quiet, real carefully
like he's talking out over a lake and
he doesn't want to risk hearing the echo

Giving Way

*like leaves frozen in the lake, like the white truck, like the ice giving
way* the water wasn't cold at first but hot hot like touching the
radiator, fingers tight, I was supposed to grab the rope, through
the ice trying to grab the rope, Mom saying *they dragged you out
by the hood of your coat*

scratchy lips breathing into mine, sometimes I think I see your
shadow tall and leaning avoiding my eyes, I remember in spots
the dark room and down the hall mice voices

truck leaving ice splitting, Daddy carrying boxes out the front
door Mom makes crackers with peanut butter and hot
chocolate, on the phone with Grandfather, her voice high and
stretched like a rubber band, like glass cracking talking about
falling through the ice

she's on the phone saying *Daddy, he's gone, no Daddy
I don't know why*

Purcell's Cove Road

if I were to say, our house collapsed in the
storm, if I were to say, the china was in
pieces, if I were to say, Daddy's voice still
echoes, even without the walls

                              you would know

that I sat days on the doorstep waiting for
him, that there aren't hurricanes in Nova
Scotia, that he didn't take everything with
him, but he tried

Daddy says he teaches people about people
but that's not really the word
I want to know the word
so when people ask me what he does
I can tell them

He won't tell me because I don't know
he thinks I won't understand
but I just want to know the word
so I can tell other people
like passing along a note I won't read
or a cup of water I won't spill

Grandmother is always getting cold, like she hasn't eaten or doesn't have anything to keep her blood flowing. cold like walking in the night when you want to be warm beside someone and the wind is cutting through your jeans

she went green, not with envy but with poison, poison in her blood. doctor Reid's face carved in wood, and he used words like degenerative and prognosis

Vera said *it was poison and envy alright, poison from a heart gone sour. that's what I say, all those years a biting words and nestling the hurt in under her nails.   too late now, yup. yup. can't just let loose, it's not her way, not even the beams a this house could take that pressure*

so the hospital people put her on a machine. her face went from green to custard to rice pudding. they call it remission but Vera said *lies split continents and settle in the hollows*

her heart sounds like an
engine trying to start, each time
almost turning over

The Sears and Roebuck House

Aunt Tory's on the porch of our Sears and Roebuck house, she rocks and shakes her head, says *he loved her something awful loved her 'til his elbows shook, 'til he couldn't sit still, 'til he was damn near crazy just watching her breathe. my poor brother Howe, he loved her alright*

when I get to press the doorbell Maya crumbles. she makes piles and drawers and says *Mine*. everything I do takes a piece away from her. this morning it was underwear. I put mine in with hers in the hamper and now she's saying she won't have any clothes. Mom says it's because Grandmother died. Maya says put a safety pin through your heart to keep it together. *it's broke* Aunt Tory says *it's broke and Howe can't fix it*. she means the doorbell.

when Grandpa couldn't hear so good, he got this doorbell to play a song. Maya says it makes us sound like the Adams family. Grandpa says it's called Pacho Bell's Canon. it went on and on so we would all hear it. Grandpa said that song was about the stones in Italy, about flying on a clear day. the thing was it was still going real loud when you answered the door. so you'd have to yell at the person.

Grandpa took the screws out and cut the tape or flicked a gear or something to fix it. he cut the song in half so it would be just going along and then it would end. Grandpa says it's better this way but he really doesn't mean it. Maya says she doesn't have enough clothes. not enough and what, could fill all that space

D-Day

I.

the sky was dark with planes, the water filled with ships

we remember—we remember things we never saw or never knew
if you hear the story enough times
you start to make the pictures, find the details:
the stoops of apartment buildings, leaning doorways, crowded
trains, starved hands through bars, hidden basements, the alleys,
the dark windows

the sky was the water

he learned to fly in Italy in go-cart planes
so many others misjudged the landing
Grandpa took pictures of the crashes, fatal/not fatal
and of a friend from Aberdeen he writes

Mickey vs. gravity

Grandpa points to the clouds just coming in
to the branches gathering wind
he sweeps his hand through the air
then brings his palm down and follows the path of a plane landing

II.

Once you've gone out in the night
you need something to guide you back
          like a porch light, a lantern or an airplane runway

when Grandmother started forgetting she made lists
      every school she ever taught at, every house she ever lived in

they'd go out in front to look back at the house
this is our house they'd say
         a searchlight, a flair, a lantern

these are your pictures:
baby Sandy, your sixth-grade class, the gray house in Denver
      a street light, a small fire, a reflection on the water

Grandpa's looking out the window
hoping the forest can tell him something
      the wedding spoon, the smell of pine, Aunt Tory's voice

when it's dinnertime, Grandmother says she's not staying
that her father's coming for her
she looks out the window to see if he's coming up the road

Christo Dios Grandpa said at the first bombing
I wouldn't have missed it for the world he said in the end

Out of the Nest

Maya's baby wakes up at the crinkle of a letter opening
or the click of a coffee cup on the table

he's like us, Mom says, *he gets hurt easily*

what Maya really hopes is that he won't be shy
and stand like her in the doorframe
between hinges and window glass

Grandfather counted five directions
north, south, east, west and here

we're fighting Mom's cancer with everything there is

she's pushing me back to school
dropping me off at the Quik Mart for the night bus

she's waving
and I'm waving back
but the bus is dark
and the station bright yellow
so all she can see is herself waving
in the row of windows passing

Lay It Down

Lay It Down

There were people in restaurants, there were bars and cigarettes
there were summer nights in parks where the lamplight made
shadows over the trees and people were kissing and summer
dresses were thin, there were people who went to concerts and
danced in high heeled shoes who groped strangers who drank too
much who woke up in the morning and had coffee with cream
and crepes and told outrageous stories of the night before

                              that wasn't me

I was looking in the windows, leaning weak against the door,
restless, swollen aching my hips unsettled
there were doctors in lab coats doctors with nice houses and cars
there were doctors with tests with theories
doctors with crystals and mood rings
there were ladies on Oprah there were strangers on the street
saying try aloe vera, vitamin B, shark fin, gingerroot

I was burnt flat out but then there was fireweed, and moss and
ferns again and after that there were parties to go to with
cosmopolitans and Cuban bands and tight dresses and night air
and the grip of a man learning to dance, coming out of it now
everything is better than I thought
the high notes, the driveway kisses, the ice cream

I was sick, I looked terrible Felt aweful i was broken down to losing
everyday was worse
so i started to let go to clean out old closets, put my shoe box of
regrets out with trash, i had to loosen up my dreams,
i had to clean out old closets, i had to loosen up dreams, i had to
not care about the places i'd left, i had to pull myself back into the
living, from a burned out forest

i amde myself a burned out forest, where everything was lost when
all the tragedy and dissapointment and the pressure of failing was

gone i laid and rested then i could rest, then i was read y to go to
give up but the fire weed came first and the moss and the ferns.
clear the way for the fireweed the moss the low lying greens

i dried out like a burned field scorached and barren then i clean
out old closets, loosened up on my dreams, i had to not care
about the places i'd left, i had to lay out with nothing
behind me and nothing before me
somehow
there was my sixteen year old car there was me with a part time
job my room in a boarding house, my family far and further away
and the sickness it was growing
i was stretchd too thin too many things lost and longing

i had to lose everything and then like a forest after the fire slowing
growing back

burned out and still

like i'd never done it before
like coming up over the edge and jumping
to the tired, exhusted from a night of parties and talking rather
than from sleepless hours

upon hours

nothing helped
the lady on opera had a different problem but one days she was
better just like walking out of a dark tunnel into light she said and
I hoped that was me

she said you had to want to be get better
but me I was stripped and bare, something inside me has tear
inside I was dried out like march after the snow when everthing
has been ded and frozen for months and I was walking across the

frozen marsh with that clear blue winter sky and
those old man bare trees walking cautious over the ice i had fallen
through over the ice i had use my mittens to pull out off over the
burning just before freezing i was walking away

i
and there were people through windows
talking on phones
there were people complaining about the service
there were people spending days in shopping malls
there were people sleeping all day
three was me in boat on the river with the current and the storm

laid out flat watching the sky there was the hum of rapids
there was breaking and the spray

it wasn't like coming out of a dark tunnel
it was more like walking on the ice
and I said oh, look at the sky clear blue of winter
look that the bare old man branches
look at this lake stretching on forever
look at me walking here where once i fell through

nothing helped i got worse and worse

i would collect straws, i would fumble with coins i would drive
home and cry, i was drying out i was empiting all the greens i'd
known all the good days were from

61

sometime when i didn't know it would end or that i'd forget how
much i'd wanted to live

i counted elements water rice air
my bones emtied I ate broth on opera they said you had to want
to get better and i i did but there was the hopelessness, the
sickness

i was laid out rock drying and brittle

and then there was the lady on opera who didn't go outside for
seven years and then she mustered up her will and thought
about outside and inside and fear and what she might be
missing like ice cream sundaes on the patio or walking in the
spary of a fountain or plum blossems that lighting through the
air across lawns over cars, sidewalks and porches,
plum blossoms the first in spring
and she said when she finally went out it was like coming out of
a dark tunnel
and maybe this could be my time of darkness and maybe some I
too could emerge

it's not quit like stepping outside
I still like in the glass the house
with the weak bones
the fragile
the lost days into years

resurfacing wanting to go back to live over all the days I lost all
my regret to redue but
pass this let this on do these things today

there were days i wanted like that

Translation

Butter Melts in Summer

Girls are showing their arms and angles and toenails

after the whip cream and frosting the lady said
Artaud is more beautiful than the beach

I should have left right then

kirei ni
to make pretty
to make clear
to mark latitude, the angle
of my body on the sidewalk
stitched and patched with moss with seaweed with lab coats

move nights by tree bark
breathe dragonflies and mosquitoes
measure longitude in holes in my skin

before this there were salmon pastries and cuff links
there were petitfours and cream buns
there was Neil Young and I was the cinnamon girl

I sleep hill and a grave of trees

I am holding up and dropping veils of morning

it's only poetry but the lady's yelling, saying that I ate her lunch

Prognosis

They are making a record of my trespasses
my mistakes and translations

I was not good enough
to balance a jar of water on my head
or to walk along the balance beam
doing cherry drops
or to look you straight in the eye

when I can't sleep Lexy tells me
about the thorns and the scratchy branches
about flying up above them into the clouds

when I can't sleep Lexy tells me
to draw a circle in chalk in the driveway
this is the world, she says
I'm bringing in sand dunes, salt ocean, soda pop,
August sun, ice cream and nothing else

I try to rest my hips and my thorny chest
and forget all the rows of numbers
the proportions of blood to water

to tell the truth
the circle's not big enough
unless you can believe
that you can bring in the ocean
which also brings in the sky
and all the trees
and the birds and beach towels and sun hats

but then I'd have to look you
straight in the eye

and when it's not dark
it's too bright
to see at all

Red Hollow

I mark days in lines on the bedpost
bathe in salt water and ice cream

please don't tell anyone about the salt
or the midnight radio
or the patterns in my blood

I believe in skiing over the rocks when the snow is thin

when my mother got cancer she said
the goal now is to die of something else

I'd be better off with faith

My father is calling Karl Marx a prophet

we danced our feet crunching in back yard snow

getting better is something to say
instead of grave or progressive

we are sword fighting in shadows on the wall
we are walking through the woods with wet mittens
we are reading the sign by the lake that says the ice will hold

I believe in throwing all my dresses off the roof

On the Coast

I forget how to measure with my hands
the length between the root cellar, the room
at the back of the house, the clothesline
and the shore

I forget the dream fish, the tooth fairies
the angel's wings on me in the night

I forget how to nestle the worry
up into my lungs
tuck my memories into the dark crevasses
with the tobacco and stale smoke

how I moved so far away, why I didn't study biology
where were the babies when these weary bones
could stay up all night

I try to remember
to feel the dry texture of breadfruit in my mouth
the sand shifting into the shape of my body
our shadows in the night while I push you to push me
out into the water
that lasts forever
and then disappears

Pigs in a Blanket

to Laverne Frith

Marina lost her Rolex at the beach

another girl lost her bikini top

Laverne's got his lotto tickets spread out all over the counter
I've got a short stack with blueberries and Cool Whip

tsuuka—an artist of clamshells
means a wealthy person

to swim in the Pacific I run into the waves and fall forward

the guy across the aisle lost teeth to highways
the night shift and bacon

beika—rice money
means American dollars

when Laverne was in school he counted
the packages of saltines that come free with a bowl of soup

I take out loans and buy red sandals
the mail comes with rows of numbers
from his apartment window my father is yelling
what's money

they're hoping for rain then sun then a late frost

the guy across the aisle wants to know who all is in my class
he says he *wants to sleep with everyone*

Yellow Wood

I have left the bed unmade
calls unanswered
my bookcase is out on the sidewalk
my wax kite flying without a string

somewhere in this body is a compass
that must realign
to metal detectors, to flight patterns, to unfurnished rooms

this is my library card
this is my plane ticket

      ippai means one cup
      ippai means I've had enough

standing on a street corner in Peterborough
the snow is coming down in April
there are two roads from here

      力一杯
      a strong cup:
      with all my might

      別れの杯をくむ
      dividing a cup and drinking:
      to leave

Read Me Where I Lie

Sensei doesn't like me changing the words
breathing my angle into them
tracing them into my shape

he wants me to tell you
love song actually means
the voices of working girls
calling to customers in the night

he wants me to tell you
you're losing a grade point
for each day that you can't decide

translate:
before and after
gathering darkness
under the shadow of clouds

the words come underwater
breathed in like air
seeded to spruce, to elm, to fir

he wants me to tell you
a different kind of love song

How to Find a Man up to the Task

This body is measured in sugar
in days of butter
in soft flour, in honey, in ground sesame

器 ki—a container
量 ryou—a measure
負 fu—to erase, to take back, to make into nothing

count me aged and aging
count me calcium and marrow and churned butter
pound me into the bedsprings
into cotton and late night radio
into dulce and kelp and dry leaves

on Barrington street, handsome
dirt in his nails and clear, strong eyes:

broke, hungry, will work
for food, beer or money

器量負け   kiryoumake

(a container) (a measure) (to make into nothing)
also means too smart for success
or too beautiful for your own good

he sees me watching him and flips over the sign:

quality sperm available
bargain price
everything included

Riverbed

If it's not yarrow laid in fields
your hands on the seam of my shirt
your eyes, a clothesline, reeling me in

then there must be a way to write a silent syllable
that measures the distance between words
or counts space in the air

if it's not the lilt of your voice
your clothes in a pile
then write this
as a pause or a dash or a skipped page
from the upstairs window into the yard
not facing up to the way our bodies become frail

Jordan, named after a river
why not some other name
a still body of water
one that could freeze and thaw
one that could take the winter back in spring

The Kite Maker

I.

This kite is bigger than the floor
wider than the streets I carry it through

> *don't move to the States*, Cormac says, *it'll ruin you*

a line between here and the sky
into the rainstorm into the thunder

I have made an attic room into boxes
my kite in shoes and wool sweaters
in mulberry paper
in meters and meters of string

> a carp swimming upstream
> = success

> pine and bamboo
> = resilience

as big as the sky
paint it orange, paint it green

> *it'll ruin you*

I let it crash into the river
I let it float out of my hands

keeping the bamboo lines to retie
into a flying crane into another city

this time a bird
this time a moth
the sky will be blue and white

II.

In Tokyo they call me the honorable foreigner
in Halifax, my hometown, they say *she's from away*

patch me words through a tin can string
send me hymns through oak tree wires

the end of the string = the highest point in the sky

these are kites my grandfather made:
Spanish rice, the screened in porch
a house with 16 beds

beds crammed into the cedar closet
roll-aways folded in under the stairs

oak tree branches = a flight path

he's in the kitchen telling my mother
make sure she knows she can always come home

light over the wingspan of a rice paper hawk
bones in strips of bamboo

I would add on a tail to make it easier to fly
but grandpa says *that kite needs to fly on its own*

III.

A haiku always has a breaking word

a kite is a kind of dream

I'll trade you two drawings for a lemon leaf

Cormac is getting married to someone else

the sound *kaku*
can mean both to write and to plough

different characters but the same sound
so one is in the other's shadow

> *Traveling all my life*
> *ploughing a small field*
> *back and forth*
>   —Basho

plum rain means the rainy season

burnt evening means a spell that breaks at dawn

I'll tow your car out of the ditch for a beer

the wind is too strong

the wind is not strong enough

Stanley Park with my Father, 2006

From dark, burrowed soil
the windstorm pulled trees right out of the ground
taking down others as they went

o-kagesama de
means *under the shade of this good tree*
and *with your help*
and *I'm fine*

he charts the potential of his body failing
makes a list
eyes, ankles, heart:
at 71 he forgets
or ignores or tries not to see
that my list is shorter
and more narrow
it will come on gradually
I will sleep in the ache
it will always be with me
but I will forget what it was like before
the frame of a building
marrow, mica, salinity

o-kagesama de
the honorable shadow
moss, lichen, mold
to lean on other trees

Layers of Damp December

This year I turn with the leaves
lay myself across the forest floor
become a home for worms
a nest for moths
harborer of millipedes, fiddleheads, mushrooms

he calls me the queen of cakes, the queen of excuses

there's meatloaf and frozen green beans
the rain is coming in sheets marking days

I am seven
his plans are paper bag lunches
his hurry a form of blindness
the lines of his shadow on the sea wall
his hands, desperate as traffic

he calls me over bark, over moss

he's remaking the edges of the story
leaving out dinners of milk over toast
of fingers callused from sewing
of leaving before the rent is due

he calls me the queen of waking dreams, the queen of lost mittens

Gravity

Lay me down on paper, wear me in a paper dress
                              cut me out of cardboard

doctor Reid furrows her brow and goes over the shadows again
trying to measure things she can't see

心   電   図

heart   rainfield   map

                                              electrocardiogram

velocity   = $\dfrac{\text{distance}}{\text{time}}$

time   = $\dfrac{\text{day}}{\text{what you remember}}$

homeless men in stoops with layers and layers of jackets on
your most credible theory on love   the migration of birds
high notes   arias   samba   eli

$\dfrac{\text{mass}}{\text{distance traveled}}$ =   the chance of my recovery

Landscape

Hang me, your honor, up with the furniture
the dictionary is out of words, out of pages

let me sleep with the shadows on the north face
let me sleep with the limestone, sleep with the ash
sleep with the winged insects captured there

let me dream the blank pages that were once a dictionary
let me run my fingers over the smooth Braille
let the images of each entry evaporate
into pockets of air of sleep of denim

the water is moving underground
there are so many of us and each desperate

I should go to Oakland
where no one has what they need
search the corners between Fruitvale and MacArthur
between High street and 73rd
for paper cups, taco shells, tootsie roll comic strips

in Japanese there's a character that means
searching for something
and a different character
that means searching for something you've lost

I open the dictionary again, still blank

Notes

I am indebted to the translations and explications of
Basho's work in Toshiharu Oseko's book, *Basho's Haiku*
(Tokyo: Oseko, 1990).

A number of the poems in this collection took shape through
Andrew N. Nelson's *Japanese-English Character Dictionary*
(Tokyo: Tuttle, 1974), which was an endlessly rich source for
tracing connections among words and characters. The Japanese
words and phrases in my work, while informed by this dictionary
and other sources, depart in many ways from standard usage.

The quote from Claude Roy that is the epigraph to the poem
Water Voices is found in *The Colors of Poetry* by Ooka Makoto
and translated by Takako U. Lento and Thomas V. Lento
(Rochester, Michigan: Katydid Books, 1991).

The title *Whale Music* comes from Paul Quarrington's book
that was made into a movie and the *Rheostatics* soundtrack
to that film.

The last stanza of *Riverbed* was inspired by a passage in
Jeanette Winterson's *Sexing the Cherry* (Vintage, 1990).

photo by Shinsuke Kiryu

Judy Halebsky is a contributing editor and translator for the bilingual poetry journal Eki Mae. Residencies at the MacDowell Colony and the Millay Colony have supported her work. Originally from Halifax, Nova Scotia, she was recently in Japan studying noh theatre on a research scholarship from the Japanese Ministry of Education (MEXT).

The New Issues Poetry Prize

Judy Halebsky, *Sky=Empty*
2009 Judge: Marvin Bell

Justin Marks, *A Million in Prizes*
2008 Judge: Carl Phillips

Sandra Beasley, *Theories of Falling*
2007 Judge: Marie Howe

Jason Bredle, *Standing in Line for the Beast*
2006 Judge: Barbara Hamby

Katie Peterson, *This One Tree*
2005 Judge: William Olsen

Kevin Boyle, *A Home for Wayward Girls*
2004 Judge: Rodney Jones

Cynie Cory, *American Girl*
Barbara Maloutas, *In a Combination of Practices*
Louise Mathias, *Lark Apprentice*
Bradley Paul, *The Obvious*
Heidi Lynn Staples, *Guess Can Gallop*
Ever Saskya, *The Porch is a Journey Different from the House*
Matthew Thorburn, *Subject to Change*
2003 Judge: Brenda Hillman

Paul Guest, *The Resurrection of the Body and the Ruin of the World*
2002 Judge: Campbell McGrath

Sarah Mangold, *Household Mechanics*
2001 Judge: C.D. Wright

Elizabeth Powell, *The Republic of Self*
2000 Judge: C.K. Williams

Joy Manesiotis, *They Sing to Her Bones*
1999 Judge: Marianne Boruch

Malena Mörling, *Ocean Avenue*
1998 Judge: Philip Levine

Marsha de la O, *Black Hope*
1997 Judge: Chase Twichell